WHATEVER HAPPENED TO THE PONY EXPRESS?

BY
Verla Kay

ILLUSTRATED BY
Kimberly Bulcken Root & Barry Root

G. P. PUTNAM'S SONS ✳ AN IMPRINT OF PENGUIN GROUP (USA) INC.

To my best friend and favorite author, Linda Joy Singleton, whose wonderful example of never giving up encouraged me to keep writing and who taught me through her fabulous books how to make my words sing to readers.
V. K.

For Elijah James Langford.
K.B.R. & B.R.

G. P. PUTNAM'S SONS
A division of Penguin Young Readers Group.
Published by The Penguin Group. Penguin Group (USA) Inc., 375 Hudson Street, New York, NY 10014, U.S.A. Penguin Group (Canada), 90 Eglinton Avenue East, Suite 700, Toronto, Ontario M4P 2Y3, Canada (a division of Pearson Penguin Canada Inc.). Penguin Books Ltd, 80 Strand, London WC2R 0RL, England. Penguin Ireland, 25 St. Stephen's Green, Dublin 2, Ireland (a division of Penguin Books Ltd.). Penguin Group (Australia), 250 Camberwell Road, Camberwell, Victoria 3124, Australia (a division of Pearson Australia Group Pty Ltd). Penguin Books India Pvt Ltd, 11 Community Centre, Panchsheel Park, New Delhi - 110 017, India. Penguin Group (NZ), 67 Apollo Drive, Rosedale, North Shore 0632, New Zealand (a division of Pearson New Zealand Ltd). Penguin Books (South Africa) (Pty) Ltd, 24 Sturdee Avenue, Rosebank, Johannesburg 2196, South Africa. Penguin Books Ltd, Registered Offices: 80 Strand, London WC2R 0RL, England.

Design by Richard Amari. Text set in Cloister.
The drawings were done in pencil on parchment, scanned and printed in sepia ink on Arches 140 lb. hot press watercolor paper, and then painted in gouache and watercolor. Kim mostly drew, Barry mostly painted, but they both did some of each.

Library of Congress Cataloging-in-Publication Data
Kay, Verla. Whatever happened to the pony express? / Verla Kay ; illustrated by Kimberly Bulcken Root and Barry Root. p. cm. Summary: A family's cross-country communication changes during the development and demise of the Pony Express. [1. Stories in rhyme. 2. Pony express—Fiction. 3. Postal service—History—Fiction.] I. Root, Kimberly Bulcken, ill. II. Root, Barry, ill. III. Title.
PZ8.3.K225Po 2010 [E]—dc22 2008053556

ISBN 978-0-399-24483-4
1 3 5 7 9 10 8 6 4 2

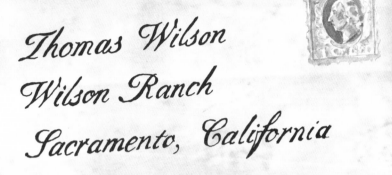

Thomas Wilson
Wilson Ranch
Sacramento, California

Brother, sister
Far apart.
Writing letters
From the heart.

Rugged country,
Mountains, sand.
Tough to travel,
Massive land.

Stagecoach, horses,
Carry mail.
Blocked by boulders,
Rough dirt trail.

Raging rivers,
Swampy spot.
Tall, steep mountains,
Desert, hot.

Send by water?
Mail by ships?
Could work better . . .
Faster trips.

Steamer chugging,
Ocean, port.
Bags of letters,
Bundles, sort.

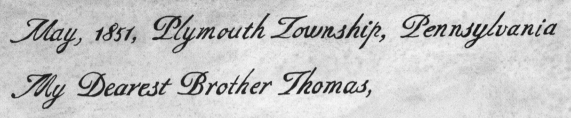

May, 1851, Plymouth Township, Pennsylvania

My Dearest Brother Thomas,

Henry Snodgrass and me got hitched up Sunday last. The weddin was real purty. You were sorely missed.

Love, Prudence

Thomas mumbles,
Grumbles, "Late!
This is old news,
Out of date."

Ponder problem,
Something new?
"Arab camels?
They might do."

Sharp rocks, desert,
Bundles sway.
Horses rearing—
"Runaway!"

Humpback camels,
Dismal test.
Sell to circus,
Free the rest.

Let's try ponies,
Cloppity-click.
With small riders,
They'll go quick.

Orphans wanted,
Riders, rough.
Risk death daily,
Must be tough.

Ponies purchased,
Mailbags, thin.
Special saddles.
"Spurs—dig in!"

Dashing riders,
Brightly dressed.
Racing swiftly,
East and west.

Dust clouds billow,
Narrow trail.
Rider guarding
Precious mail.

Arrows twanging,
War whoops, cry.
Rider races,
Gallops by.

Letters, papers,
"Must get through."
Lonely outpost,
Rendezvous.

Stationmaster,
Midnight sky.
Changing horses
"On the fly."

Town of buildings,
Rider, spy.
Townsfolk cheering,
Hats thrown high!

July, 1860, Sacramento, California

Dear Prudence,

It were twins again! Doc says Charity's plum wore out with seven girls now and cain't have no more. Reckon I'll be gettin some hired hands soon to help with the ranch, cause it's doin great—too much work fer jest me and no boys of my own to help out.

Love, Thomas

August, 1860, Plymouth Township, Pennsylvania

Dear Thomas,

We was surprised (and happy!) to hear from you so quick. Sorry to hear bout Charity, specially since we jest had ourselves another fine strapping boy.
We named this'n Tom after you. Someday he'll work in the mine like his Pa.

Love, Prudence

Holes for wood poles,
Digging down.
Long wires stretching,
Town to town.

No more ponies,
Fired staff.
Faster news now—
Telegraph.

Send a message,
Morse code, use.
Tap, tap, tapping,
Instant news.

To Thomas Wilson   Date September 10, 1862

By Telegraph from   Prudence Snodgrass

Accident in the mine yesterday. Oldest boy Jimmy died.
Pa having trouble breathing from coal dust. I'm scared
for the rest of my boys. Wish they weren't in the mine.

Prudence

Parcels, letters,
Go by trail.
Less expensive,
Slower mail.

Stagecoach thunders,
Rumbles near.
Coachman hollers,
"Mail is here!"

August, 1869

Plymouth Township, Pennsylvania

Dear Unkle Thomas,

  Thank you fer the purty knife. Now I'm 9, Pa set me to workin in the coal mine. I hav to pick rocks out of the coal. Its hard work and dirty to. I liked schol beter. Wish I could work on the ranch with you, instead.

    Love, Tom

New-built train tracks,
Shiny rail.
Freight cars loaded,
Stuffed with mail.

Whistle blowing,
Smoky smell.
High-pitched screeching,
Clanging bell.

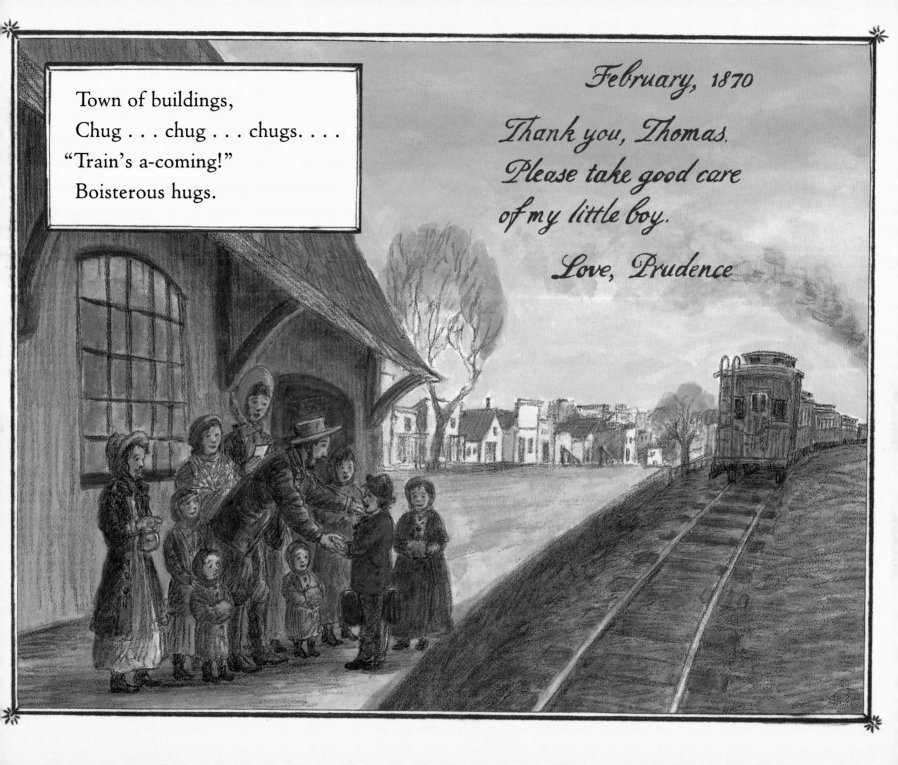

Town of buildings,
Chug . . . chug . . . chugs. . . .
"Train's a-coming!"
Boisterous hugs.

February, 1870

Thank you, Thomas.
Please take good care
of my little boy.

Love, Prudence

Outpost, station,
Roofline sags.
No more ponies,
Riders, bags.

Now they're empty,
Trains chug past.
Mail and people,
Moving fast.

AUTHOR'S NOTE

When our country was first formed, mail was hand-delivered. A letter would be given to a friend, a sea captain, or a traveler with hopes it would someday reach the person to whom it was addressed. In the 1700s Benjamin Franklin started a more dependable mail service using wagons. But travel across this vast, rugged land was difficult because of its rough terrain, high mountains and raging rivers, making it very difficult for families living far apart to get news in a timely manner. It took so long to cross the country in 1854 that a popular joke was that a senator or congressman from California might find his term of office had ended before he reached our country's capital! Mail was sent by steamships, stagecoaches and even camels, in an effort to find a reliable, fast way to communicate across the country.

The Pony Express (which used small, strong, fast horses, not ponies as we know them today) was created to quickly transport important letters and messages to and from the West Coast. The Pony Express trail ran between St. Joseph, Missouri, and Sacramento, California, from April 3, 1860, to October 26, 1861. Riders changed horses at depots every 10 to 15 miles along the route, taking no more than two minutes to dismount, remove the specially made lightweight mail pouches (called *mochilas*) from their saddles, remount their fresh horses and continue racing on their way. The mochila was passed to a fresh rider about every 100 miles. Mail went to and from the Pacific Coast in ten days—more than twice as fast as by stagecoach! The Pony Express was officially shut down two days after telegraph lines were completed, because messages could then be transmitted instantly from coast to coast using Morse code. To see a map of the route and locations of the depots, visit http://cprr.org/Museum/Maps/Pony_Express.html

Overland mail and packages were then delivered by trains and stagecoaches. These methods of mail delivery eventually gave way to airplanes, and today we use a combination of jets and land vehicles to get our physical mail. Major changes in the way people communicate have occurred since the creation of cell phones, the Internet and e-mail. Today people can instantly send messages around the entire world. What changes might tomorrow bring? Only time will tell.

NOTABLE DATES

Pre-1775 Mail delivered by hand through acquaintances.

1775 Benjamin Franklin named first Postmaster General by the Continental Congress. Mail delivered by weekly mail wagons.

1823 Congress designates navigable waters as post roads. Mail sent by ship.

1849–1869 Stagecoaches used by private enterprises to carry mail and freight from coast to coast.

1853 Jefferson Davis proposes using camels to carry mail, freight, and other communications between military posts as an experiment.

May 14, 1856 Thirty-four camels arrive in the United States.

April 3, 1860 Pony Express service begins.

October 24, 1861 Telegraph line between Washington and San Francisco completed.

October 26, 1861 Pony Express officially discontinued.

February 1864 The last camels sold or turned loose.

May 10, 1869 Transcontinental railroad completed at Promontory Summit, Utah, allowing rail mail service from coast to coast.